The Workman's Sure Guide, A New System Of Handrailing...

Joseph Riley (of Leeds.)

Revised and Corrected.

The Workman's Sure Guide,

BEING A NEW SYSTEM OF

HANDRAILING,

FOR WHICH THE AUTHOR OBTAINED A FIRST-CLASS PRIZE AT THE LATE WAKEFIELD INDUSTRIAL AND FINE ART EXHIBITION.

BY

JOSEPH RILEY,

LEEDS.

SECOND EDITION.

ENTERED AT STATIONERS' HALL.

1870.

PREFACE.

In consequence of numerous enquiries from members of the trade, I have decided to issue a Second Edition, revised and corrected, with many additions and improvements never before published. To those friends who, by their generous support, contributed to the success of the First Edition, I tender my sincere thanks, and trust the present issue will supply the wants and gain the approval of all interested in its study.

J. RILEY.

Leeds, January, 1870.

HANDRAILING

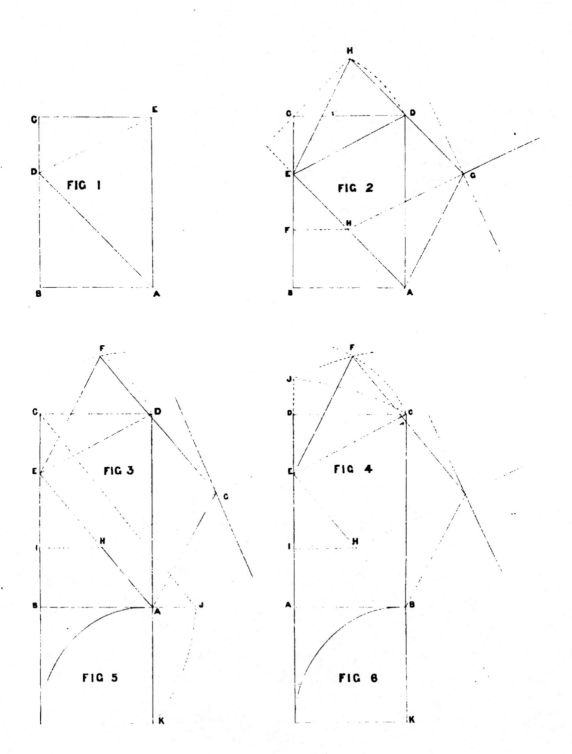

PLATE 1

Shews how to get the development of a block. .

Take a piece of square wood, cut it as fig. 1 to two pitches, after you have cut it, it forms a figure as A E H G in fig. 2 which is the development of the two pitches.

This development can be got several ways. First take fig. 2, suppose A B E be one pitch, and E C D be the other, run a line along A E, then square from that cutting the corner at C, then set the compasses at E and draw the line D H, and where it crosses the line, C H gives the covering line. Then make H G parallel to E A, and A G parallel to E H, gives the development. Then set B F equal to E C, run it to H and from H to G gives the trammel line.

Fig. 3. shews another way, set up your pitches as fig. 2.; fig. 5, shews the end of the block, set your compasses at B and make the line K J, then set the compasses from J to C, then set one leg at A and make the dotted line at F, then set the compasses from E to D and cross the line at F gives the covering line E F, make F G parallel to E A and A G parallel to E F, set B I equal to E C, run it to H and from H G gives the trammel line.

Fig. 4. shews another way, set out as before, set the compasses from A to C and make the line C J, then set the compasses from B J and make the line J F, then set the compasses at E and draw the line C F, and where they cross gives the covering line, set the top pitch at the bottom gives the trammel line. I have adopted fig. 2 as the best, simply getting a square line from A E, cutting the corner at C, and doing away with the extra lines as shewn in the others.

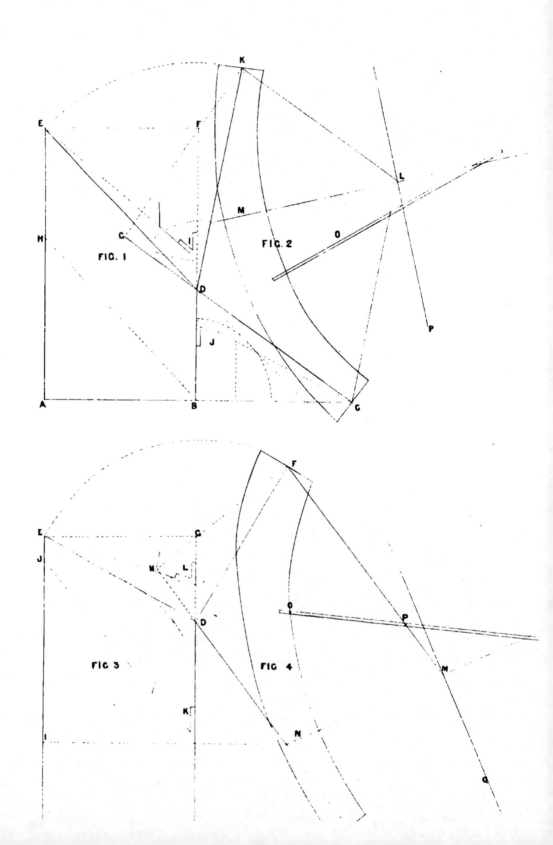

FIG. 1

FIG. 2

FIG 3

FIG 4

PLATE 2.

Shews the method of getting the face mould for twisting, how to get the bevels, and how to set the trammel,

Suppose A B on fig. 1 be the centre of rail, extend an equal distance to C, which shews the two sides or pitches. Suppose B C D be one pitch, and A B E D be the other; make a square line from E to F, then F D B, run the line C D to G, then square from that cutting the corner at F to K, then set your compasses at D, and make the line E K; and where the lines E K and G F K meet, gives the centre or covering line D K; then D K C is the centre of rail or covering lines

To get the bevels, extend the line C D to G, set the compasses at F, and make the line G I to the line B F, then I to E gives the bottom bevel. Then extend the line E D to the base line A B C, then describe the line from centre B as shewn, gives the top bevel.

To set the trammel, make the line from B to H parallel to E D, then make a square from H to the line E D, then set the compasses at D, and take it forward to the covering line D K, then from the line D K draw M L, then the line L P square from M L, gives the trammel lines Remember K L is parallel to D C, and K D is parallel to B C. To set the trammel, set the width of the rail at M then measure what width the mould wants to be at each end, which you will find by marking the width of the rail parallel to the line F D B, then measure on the bevel, gives the width. Mark them on the mould fig. 2, set the rod and strike them, and the mould is complete. For applying the mould, see Plate 3. Fig 3 and fig. 4 are got the same way.

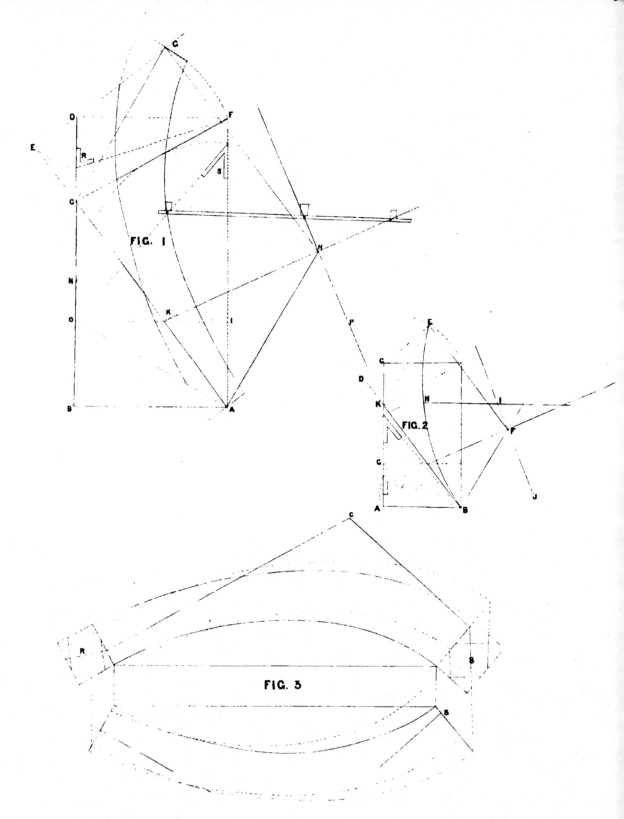

FIG. 1

FIG. 2

FIG. 3

PLATE 3.

Method of getting a face mould, and how to apply the mould to the plank.

Fig. 1.—Suppose B A be the centre of rail, the only difference between this Plate and Plate 2 is that Plate 2 is fully developed and this is not, only having the pitches in the centre of rail. Suppose B A C be one pitch, and C D F the other, extend the line A C to E, then square from that cutting D to G, then the line F G from centre C gives the centre or covering line G C, then make the line G H parallel to C A, and the line A H parallel to C G.

To get the bevels, set the compasses at D, and run it from E to R then from R to F, gives the bottom bevel R. For the top bevel, set the compasses at I to the line C F, run it to the line F A, then from O gives the top bevel S. To get the width of the mould at the ends mark the width of the rail parallel to the lines A F and B D, as shewn, measure on the bevel gives the width of the mould. Remember, it is always the width of the rail on the tranmel line K H.

To set the trammel, always set the top pitch at the bottom, that is A B O is equal to C D F, then run a square line from D B from O to the line A C, then from K to H, then H P square from K H gives how to set the trammel.

For the face mould, set the width of the rail at K, the dot being the centre of the rail then take the width at the bevel, S gives the width at the top. The bevel R gives the width at the bottom. Set the trammel, strike them, and the mould is ready.

Fig. 3.—Shews how to apply the mould to the plank. First cut the rail out square through the planks, shoot the ends, set the size of the rail out as shewn to the bevels, then apply the mould, moving while the centre lines on the mould correspond with the bevels on each end, then mark it. Place the mould on the underside, the same way as the top, moving while the centre lines on the mould correspond with those on the plank, gives the twisting lines to work to.

Fig. 2.—Shews the same as fig. 1, half-size, with the bevels got another way. Set the compasses at F, square to the line K E, then mark the same distance from B, up the line A C, gives the top bevel. Then set the compasses at F, square to the line B K, then set it up from B, the same way up the line A C, gives the bottom bevel

The trammel can be set to all the Plates in this work, as the centre lines of rails are all got the same way, by setting it as shewn in this Plate.

To set the rod and pins, is simple,—first set the two first pins to the centre or inside of the rail, as you think proper, if to the centre, place one pin at G, in fig, 1, and the other on the trammel line, and where it cuts the other line, gives the place for the other pin. Remember, get the proper widths of the mould, one end is only required, as the rod will give the other; yet it is safer for a learner to get all the widths and work to all three.

PLATE 4

METHOD OF GETTING A FACE MOULD AND BAVILS
FOR A RAIL IN AN ACUTE ANGLE.

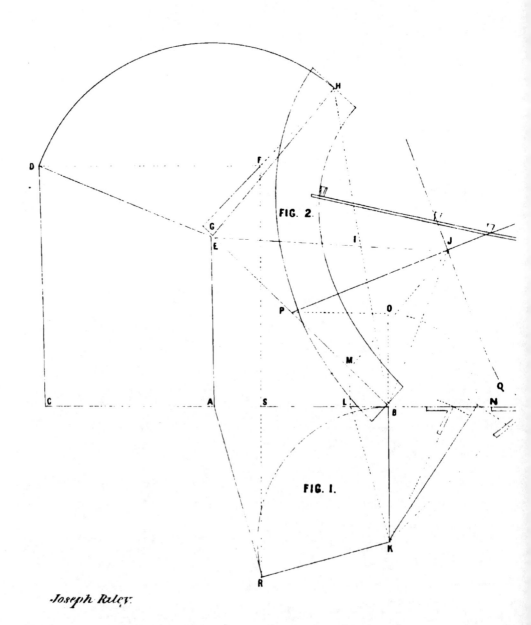

FIG. 2.

FIG. I.

Joseph Raley.

PLATE 4.

Method of getting a face mould, and bevels for a rail, in an acute angle.

Suppose Fig. 1 be the angle and centre of rail, extend the line A B to C make A C equal to A B. Set your first pitch up from A to E, then draw the line E B; then set your second pitch up from C to D, then draw the line D G; draw the dotted line D F and F R, then draw a square line from line E B, cutting the corner at F; then set your compasses at G, and draw the line from D to H, and where it cuts the line F H, gives the covering line G H, or centre of rail. Draw the dotted line H B, half it, as at I, then draw the line G J, cutting at I, then make the dotted line L K parallel to A R, then square up to the pitch line B E, then make M J parallel to G H into the line P J gives the point for the trammel. Then set your compasses from B to J, then mark the same distance from K to N, then set your compasses at B, and draw the line N O, then square to P, then from P to J, and square from P J draw J Q gives the trammel.

To get the bevel, set the compasses from J to the line G H, then from K to the line B, N gives the top bevel. To get the bottom bevel, set the compasses from J to the line B E, then from K to the line B N, gives the bottom bevel

If for a quarter pace, set up one step from C to D, and ease the shanks as in Plate 7. If for winders set it out as Plate 8, for easing and shank.

TO APPLY THE MOULD SEE PLATE 3.

METHOD OF GETTING OUT CAPS AND KNEES FOR ACUTE AND OBTUSE ANGLES

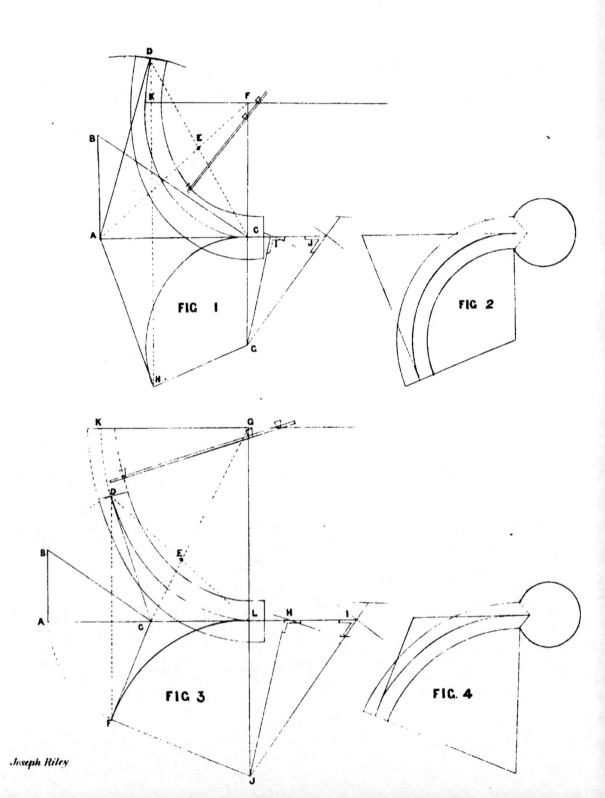

FIG 1

FIG 2

FIG 3

FIG. 4

Joseph Riley

PLATE 5.

Method of getting out caps and knees for acute and obtuse angles.

Suppose fig 2 be the Plan of the rail on the acute angle, set fig. 1 out to the angle. Suppose A B C be the pitch board, make F C square to A C then make H D parallel to F C, then set the compass from B C, then mark the same distance from A to D, and where it cuts the line H D gives the covering or centre line of rail A D. Then draw the dotted line D C, half it, as at E, then the dotted line A E, and where it cuts the line F C, gives the place to set the trammel.

To get the bevel, set the compass from F C, then from G to J on the base line gives the bottom bevel; then set the compass from F to the line A D, then set the compass at G, and make the line I on the base line gives the top bevel.

Fig. 4 is the Plan of the rail on the obtuse angle.

Fig. 3 is the method of getting the face mould. Extend the base line L C to A, set the compass at C, and draw the dotted line from F to A; then suppose A B C be the pitch Board, then make the dotted line F D, then set the compass C and draw the dotted line B D, and where the two cuts, gives the centre or covering line C D; then draw the dotted line D L, half it, as at E, then draw the line C E, extend it to the line L G, and where the two cuts, gives the place to set the trammel.

The bevels are got as in fig. 1.

To set the trammel rod, take fig. 1 first, set the first and second pins from C to G, then the first and third from C to F, will give the the centre of rail; set the width of the rail on the base line A C, then measure on the bevels gives the width of the face mould at each end. Fig. 3 is got the same way.

To apply the mould to the plank, see plate 3.

SCROLL WITH FACE MOULD

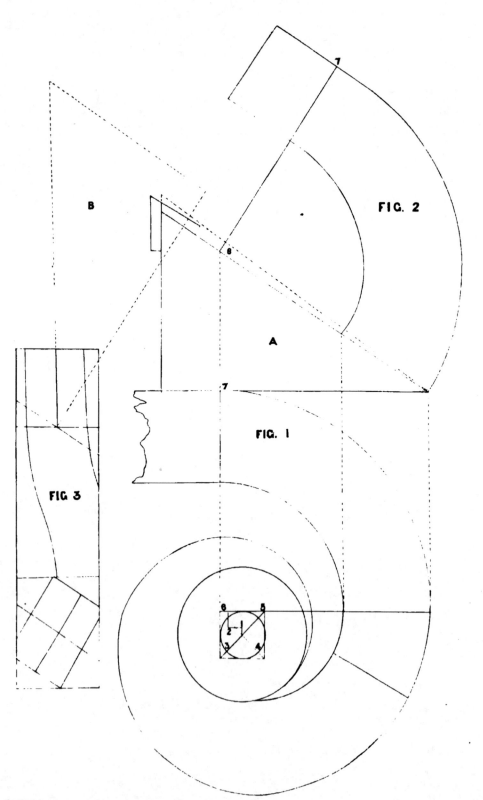

FIG. 2

B

A

FIG. 1

FIG 3

PLATE 6

Shews how to draw a scroll with face mould, and how to apply the levels to the shank.

Fig. 1 shews how to draw a scroll. Draw the cap first, then form a square, one third the diameter of the cap, then draw the lines from each corner of the square, cutting the centre of the cap, then draw the circle inside of the square, then raise the line from the centre to 1, then raise the line 2, cutting where the cross line and the inner circle meet, then draw the line 2, 1 gives all the points. First set your compass at 1, and to the underside of the cap draw your first quarter; than at 2, 3, 4, 5, 6, which completes the outside, then set your compass from 5 to the underside of the cap, draw your line 5 to the line 5, 6, extended, then from 6 to that completes the scroll, the line 6, 5, gives the joint.

Fig. 2 shews the face mould. First place your pitch board as shewn; do not draw to your pitch, but set it as shewn, about three quarters of an inch below the proper pitch, to get the curve better; trace it up from the scroll, as shewn, with your dotted lines, and what it is from 6, 7, set up the same from the pitch board 6, 7, then draw the dotted lines from the joints, gives the points to draw the face mould from.

Fig. 3 shews the shank with the pitch board applied. When you cut your plank, cut it square through. Fig. 3 shews plank on the edge. Mark all the lines from your face mould on your plank, get half the thickness of your plank, then take your bevel, as shewn in fig 2, apply it to the shank in fig. 3, then draw the dotted line square from that, is the underside of your pitch board B, which must be the proper pitch board; draw your pitch line, then add half the thickness of the rail each side, gives the rail lines to work to; then apply the bevel to the joint, mark the rail, as shewn, place your face mould on the top of the plank, so that your lines on the face mould, and the bevel lines on the shank correspond then mark your face mould all round, then place it at the underside, drawing the face mould to correspond with the bevel lines, gives, when marked, the true lines to twist from.

PLATE 7

HANDRAILING
TWIST FOR A HALF PACE

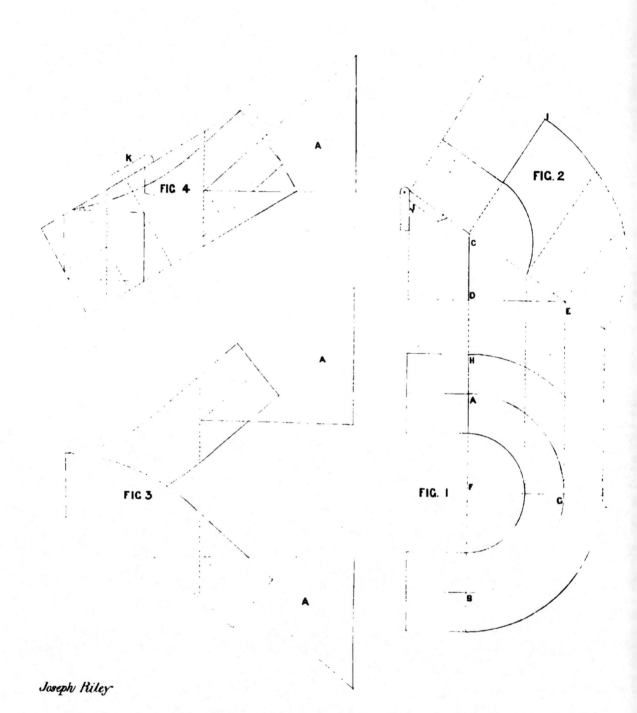

Joseph Riley

PLATE 7

Shews how to get out a rail for a half pace.   First get the centre of rail.

Fig. 1 shews the rail.   Let A B be the centre of rail; add half the with of the rail each side, trace the dotted lines up to the pitch board.

G E gives the centre of rail.   F C gives the springing.   To get the proper pitch, let D C be half the rise of the pitch board, then draw the line from E to C, gives the proper pitch, then set C I equal to F H, then the width of the rail, trace the dotted lines, gives the points to draw the face mould; then cut your shanks out to form your twist square through the plank, then take the bevel J, apply to fig. 4, as shewn, first making your square marks, as shewn, from the face mould, then take half the thickness of the rail, apply the bevel K, as shewn, then apply the pitch board A, gives the rake into the straight rail, which only wants easing from thence to the joint; then bolt the two together, forms the twist.

Fig. 3 shews the twist put together, with the pitch boards applied.

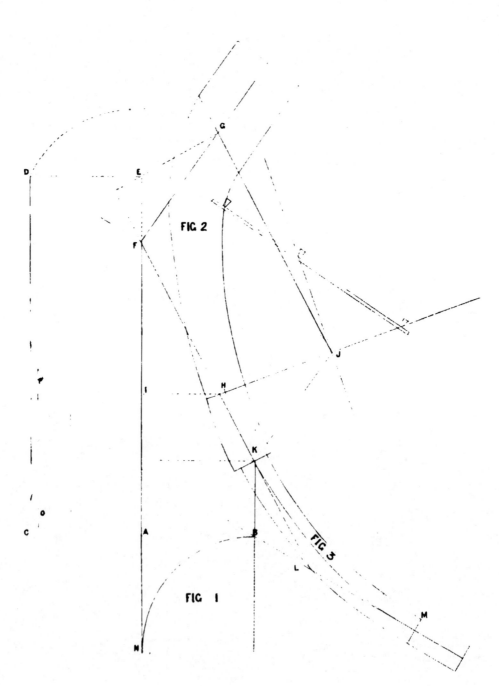

FIG 2

FIG 3

FIG 1

Joseph Riley

PLATE 8

Method of getting out a Rail for three or four winders in the Quadrant.

Suppose Fig. 1 be the centre of rail, open A N to A C, set up the height of three or four winders, as it may be up the line C D, make D F and B M your common pitches, then make the line F L crossing the springing line at K while K L is about eight inches, and L M the same, gives the easing as shewn, add four inches of straight at the bottom, then make a square line from F K, cutting the corner at E to G, then set the compasses at F and make the line D G, and where they cross, gives the covering line; make G J parallel to K F and K J parallel to F G, gives the development; set the top pitch at the bottom, gives the line, I H and from H to J gives the trammel line.

To get the bevel, set the compasses at J to the line F G square across, then set one leg at A, up the line C D gives the top bevel P, then set one leg at J to the line F K, and place one leg at A and cross the line C D, gives the bottom bevel, set the width of the rail on the bevels, and what they measure on the bevels gives the width of the face mould at each end.

For applying the mould see Plate 3.

FIG 3

FIG 2

FIG 1

PLATE 9.

Method of getting out a Rail for three winders, finishing on a level landing.

Suppose A B be the centre of a rail, as in Fig. 1, set up the height of three winders up the centre line, then allow the height you want it on the landing, that is, suppose up to C be two feet eight inches, and you want it to be three feet on the landing, add four inches more, that will make A D the full height, then make the line D E, cutting at C then E L, while L K L M are eight inches each, add a shank as shewn, gives the easing.

To get the first twist make a square line from K E, cutting the corner at O to F, then set the compasses from E to C, and make the line C F, and where they cross gives the covering line. Make F H parallel to K E, and K H parallel to E F gives the development. Set the top pitch at the bottom at I, G to H gives the trammel.

To get the bevels, set the compasses at H, to the line E F, square across, and set one leg at B, and mark up the middle line at S gives the top bevel. Then set the compasses at H, to the line K E, then set one leg at B, and cross the middle line at R, gives the bottom bevel. Set the width of the rail and mark on the bevels gives the width of the face mould at each end.

To get the top twist, set the compasses at D, and make the line C P, gives the covering line. Set the width of the rail on the bevel, and what it is, mark it on the top, strike it with the trammel, and it is ready.

Remember, add a shank at the top end. You must get parallel face moulds to cut out your stuff, in almost all cases. The thickness of the plank must be the width of the rail.

METHOD OF GETTING OUT A RAIL WHERE THREE WINDERS & A QUARTER PACE IS IN THE WELL

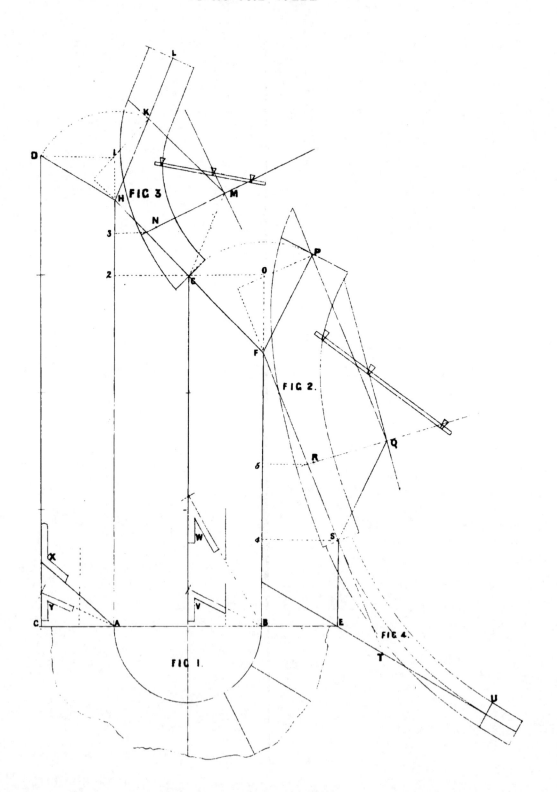

Joseph Riley

PLATE 10.

Method of getting out a Rail where three winders and a quarterpace are in the well.

Suppose A B be the centre of rail, then set up the centre line to the height of three risers at G, then from C to D, the height of four risers, apply the common pitch at D and E, then run a line from H to F, cutting at G, then from F S to T, while it is eight inches from S to T and the same from T to U, which gives the easing as shewn.

To get the face mould, make a square line from S F, cutting the corner at O to P, then set the compasses at F, and make the line G P, and where they cross gives the covering line F P, set P Q equal to F S, and S Q equal to F P, gives the development.

To get the bevels, set the compasses at Q to the line F P square across, then set one leg at B and mark up the middle line, gives the bevel W. Then set in like manner at Q, to the line S F, square across, set one leg at B, and mark in like manner, gives the bevel V. Set the width of the Rail, as shewn, and measure on the bevel, gives the width of each end of the face mould.

To get the top face mould, set a square line from G H, cutting the corner I to K, then set the compasses at H, and make the line D K, and where they cross, gives the line H K, which is the covering line. Then set K M parallel to H G, and G M parallel to H K, gives the development.

To get the bevels, set the compasses at M to the line H K, square, and set one leg at A, up the line C D, gives the top bevel X. Set again in like manner at M to line H G and mark in like manner from A, gives the bottom bevel Y. Set the width of the Rail and measure on the bevel, gives the width of each end of the face mould. Remember, add four inches of straight to the top twist for top shank, as K L.

To apply the mould, see Plate 3.

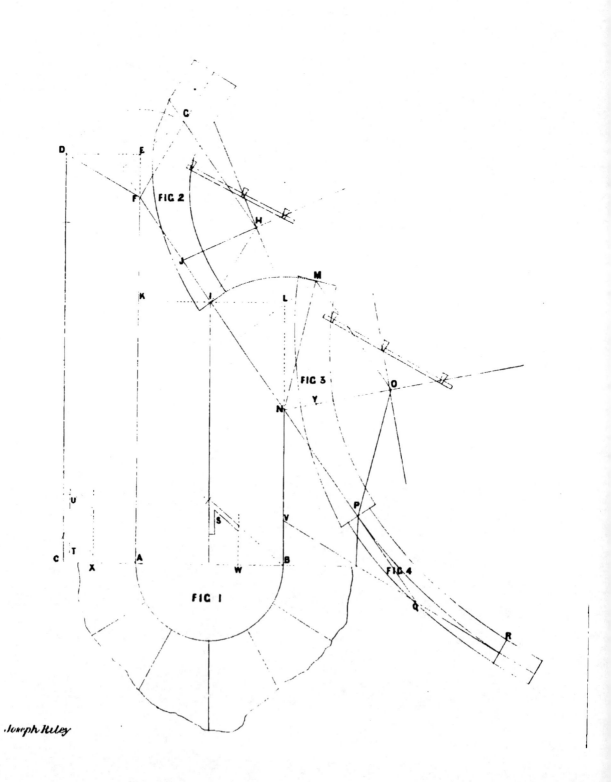

FIG 2

FIG 3

FIG 4

FIG 1

Joseph Riley

PLATE 11.

Method of getting out a Rail, for Six winders in the well.

Suppose A B be the centre of Rail, set six risers up C D, set the common pitch from D to F, and from V to Q, extending downwards, then make the line from Q to F, gives the line of the rail, make an easing at the bottom, say eight inches each way and four inches of shank, as shewn, then make the dotted line K L, cutting the pitch line at I, then make a square line from I P, cutting the corner at L, then set the compasses from N to I, and make the line I M, and where they cross gives the line M N; then make M O parallel to N P, and P O parallel to M N, gives the development for striking with the trammel.

For the top twist make the square line, from I F, cutting the corner at E to G, then set the compasses at F and make the line D G, gives the covering line; make the line G H parallel to F I, and I H parallel to F G, gives the development. Set the top pitch at the bottom, gives the trammel line The trammel line in fig. 3 is taken from the centre in consequence of their being equal pitches. Mind, allow a shank at the top of the top twist, about four inches long.

To get the bevels, set the compasses in fig. 3 from O to N M, square across, then set one leg at B, and make a line up the middle line, as shewn, gives the bevel S. Set the width of the Rail, as at W, and what it measures on the bevel is the width at P and M. Remember, it is always the width of the Rail on the trammel line. For the top bevels, set the compasses at H to the line F G, square across and mark up the line C D, gives the bevel U; then set the compasses from H to the line I F, and mark up the line C D from A, gives the bevel T or bottom bevel.

PLATE 12

METHOD OF GETTING OUT A RAIL FOR THREE WINDERS IN AN OBTUSE ANGLE

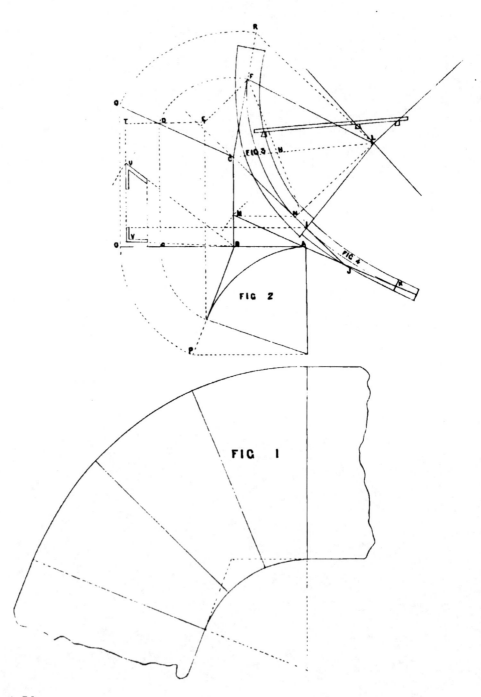

FIG 2

FIG 1

Joseph Riley

PLATE 12.

Method of getting out a Rail for three winders, in an obtuse angle.

First, set out the stairs, as fig. 1, get the angle as fig. 2, make B C equal to A B, then set the height from C to D, set the pitches top and bottom, as A B M and G D, then run a line from G to J, then set J K equal to J I, ease it as shewn, add half the thickness of the Rail each side gives fig. 4, allow four inches of straight for the shank.

To get the face mould, set a square line from I G, cutting the centre at E to F, then set the compasses at G. and make the line D F, gives the covering line G F, which is the centre of rail. To get the other lines of the development, set the compasses at B and make the line P O, run it up to Q, then set the compasses at G, and make the line Q R, then make R Y parallel to G I, than make the dotted line from I to F, half it, as at H, then draw the line G H to the line R Y, gives the lines F Y and I Y, which is the development.

To get the trammel lines, set the compasses from F to Y, mark the same distance from T to M, then run M to N, then from N to Y. Set the width of the Rail at N, then get the width at both ends from the bevels, draw it out with the trammel, which produces the face mould. Fig. 3.

To get the bevels, set the longest side of fig. 2 from B to V, then set the compasses from Y to the line G F, then mark from B U, gives the top bevels, then the same from Y to I G, mark the same way from B to V, gives the bottom bevel.

Lightning Source UK Ltd.
Milton Keynes UK
UKOW021952090113

204670UK00004B/144/P